Conter ⸀

GW01551067

Introduction ....

1 Ratby Burroughs, Thornton Reservoir ....

2 Mount St. Bernard's Abbey & Whitwick 10

3 Barrow, Woodthorpe and Quorn...15

4 Hungarton, Cold Newton, Old Ingarsby, Keyham 19

5 Birstall, Watermead & Abbey Park - A flat route by rivers and canals 26

6 Ratby, Groby Pool & Martinshaw Woods 32

7 Newtown Linford, Ulverscroft and Copt Oak 36

8 Saxelbye, Grimston, Old Dalby & Wartnaby 40

9 Gaddesby, Ashby Folville, Thorpe Satchville & Barsby 45

10 Twyford, Burrough on the Hill, Somerby & John O'Gaunt 51

Interactive Maps 56

Amendments to Volume 1 56

Great Runningand Walking Routes in Leicestershire

Volume 2

ISBN: 978-1-910181-56-0

Published by Anchor Print Group Ltd

Published in Great Britain by the Anchor Print Group Ltd

First edition published in June 2018

Introduction

Firstly, may I say a big thankyou to all of those people who purchased Volume 1. It was mainly as a result of having so much positive feedback of how you enjoyed doing the routes etc. that I decided to definitely go ahead with Volume 2.

The format seems to have been well received, especially the photos which you said gave the occasional reassurance of being in the right place, and therefore I have included more of them this time. I also know that the routes have been used by people walking them too, so, having a shorter option seemed a good choice.

I did get some comments about most of the routes being in the north of Leicestershire, so I have tried to go east and west a little more this time, but the south is still lacking I'm afraid, mainly due to not knowing that area so well.

Once again I have included some bits of history on the routes (bold & italics), even though I do get some stick from fellow Wreake Runners when we repeatedly pass these places !! (Comments like – 'On no, here we go again', or, 'Tell us again what it was like here in the 18th century Dave' !)

The analytics on the Plot-a-Route website show me that the interactive maps have been useful to you, so these are available again for these new routes to view or download to your GPS, Smartphone or Tablet.

I know I mentioned before about being prepared for diversions being made after going to print, but I didn't expect Highways Department to remove a Spot Island, as happened in Route 3 in Volume 1; and Old Rise Rocks Cottage (Route 2) to be completely demolished, changing the path down off Bardon Hill. So, after all, it was a valid point and I dare say will apply at sometime to Volume 2. (Always a good idea to have an OS map with you as well). These amendments are also included near the back of this book.

And finally, just a couple of acknowledgments. My thanks go to Richard Linnett at Anchor Print (Syston) for all his help with the maps and publishing expertise. Also to those who have accompanied me when checking out some of the routes (especially through all the mud we've had this year !) and my wife Lyn for keeping an eye on my grammar and for putting up with me either on the computer, or nipping off to take more photos of the routes.

Run or Walk, but more importantly, ENJOY !

Dave Palmer

Route 1 – Ratby Burroughs & Thornton Reservoir.

Start: Ratby Burroughs, small car park on the right along a tarmaced lane. (Burroughs Road) (LE6 0XV + 0.5 mile)

Distance: 7.75 miles (shorter option 4.75 miles)

Refreshments: The Plough Inn or Bulls Head in Ratby

1 Leave the car park by taking the gate on the right hand side of the car park. (A) After only a short distance, ignore the path that goes right and instead go left across an open field.

There is a right fork to the next yellow post and then follow the yellow posts through the trees. The metal gate ahead leads to a track going straight across you, between fences; turn right. When there is a hedge in front of you, turn right and then immediately left. (B) Eventually you reach a gate (houses on your right) which leads through to a gravel track.

Carry on straight ahead, down the gravel path, (C) looking out for the yellow post in the hedge on your left, turn here **2** . Go down the field, heading for the yellow post in the opposite diagonal corner. Continue along with the hedge on your right until you can turn right at the yellow post in the hedge **3** .

Shorter route: almost immediately take the grassy path on your left with hedges now on your left. This is now well signed with yellow posts and you eventually reach a road. Turn left, cross over and take the path through the hedge on your right (D). Go over one field and then diagonally left to a stile in the hedge to come out onto the road. Turn right and continue at **8** .

Longer route: Take the path straight ahead up towards the house. Where the path bends round to the right, take the footpath through the gate. Turn left and go diagonally across the field towards the trees. Bear right and go down the slope, noting the lake on your right. Go through the trees at the bottom, bearing left to reach a gate on your right which you go through. **4**

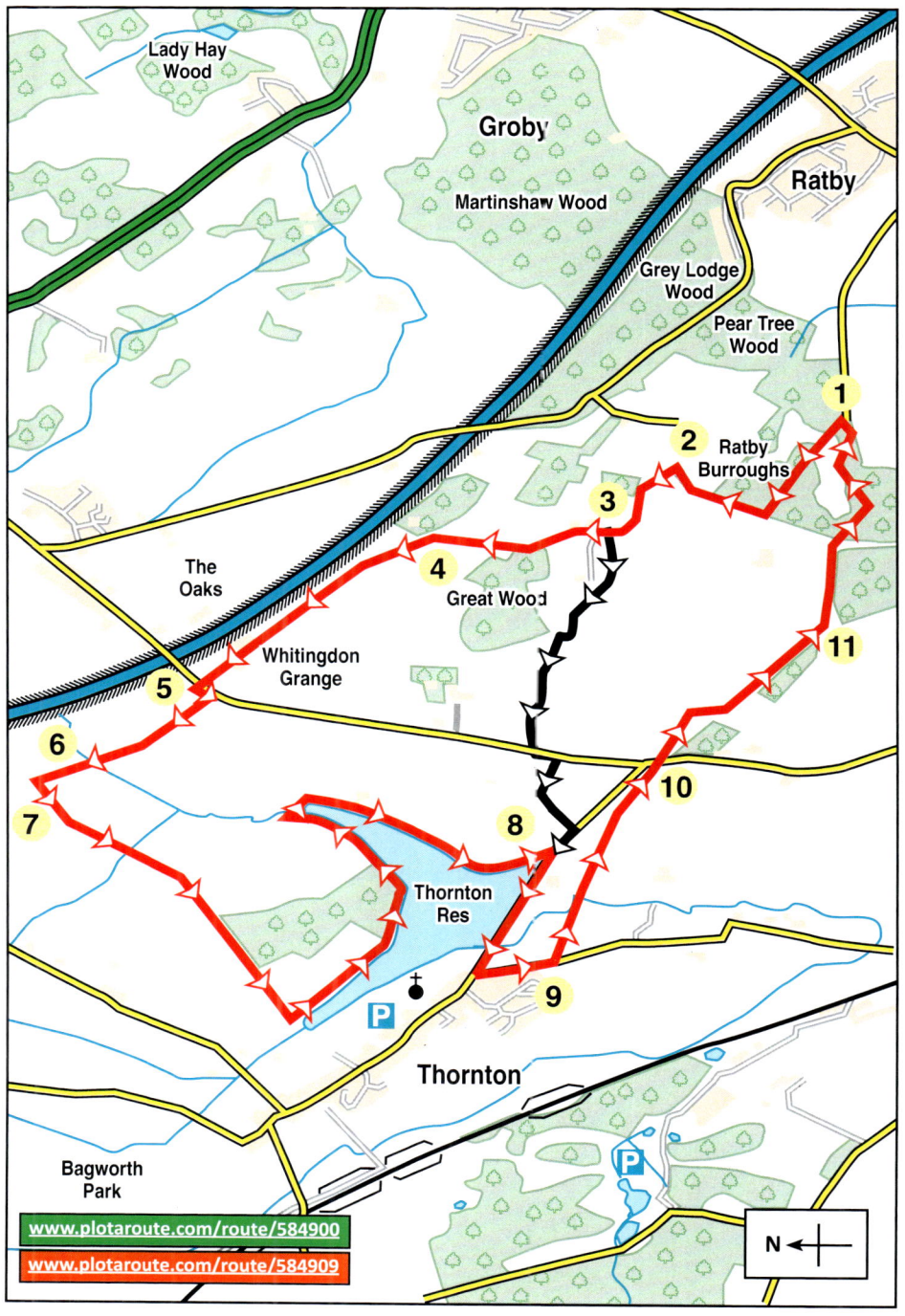

Lady Hay Wood

Groby

Ratby

Martinshaw Wood

Grey Lodge Wood

Pear Tree Wood

1

2 Ratby Burroughs

3

The Oaks

4

Great Wood

Whitingdon Grange

5

6

7

8

10

11

Thornton Res

9

Thornton

Bagworth Park

N

Going straight ahead here would take you over the motorway, but our path goes left through a squeeze style (E). The going can sometimes be awkward here with long grass but the path is obvious. At the end of this section you emerge onto a path that goes past the buildings and down their drive to the road. **5**

The next footpath is across the road to the left (F). Continue along this path until it descends into the last field and then you need to cross half right to the yellow post (G) where a narrow bridge takes you over a stream into trees. **6**

The path here twists and turns through the trees, but eventually comes out in a wide clearing where you head left. After only a distance of about 100 m, look for a yellow post on your left in the trees. This is a crossroads of paths. **7**

Turn left and climb up the bank to reach an open field, continue straight ahead and then path goes down (H) to a small metal gate on the right of the larger metal gate. (Ignore the stile on your right) Go through this smaller gate and climb the hill in front of you, keeping the hedge on your right.

A short distance over the top, look for a metal gate in the hedge and take this, but the path then still heads in the same direction so the hedge is now on your left. Proceed ahead and you eventually descend.

One more gate on the left to look out for and go through (although there is a stile just before it which could be taken). Turn right and continue to reach the northerly tip of Thornton reservoir. Go left here (I) and follow the gravel path that goes clockwise round the reservoir until you eventually reach the road. Turn right.

8 Keep on the road alongside the reservoir (J), up the slope to the T junction and then turn left.

Stay on the left hand side and take the **first** footpath through the hedge on your left. **9** (K)

Thornton Reservoir was originally built in 1854 when it had its own treatment works which were situated to the south of the current dam. It is now owned by Severn Trent and the water is treated a few miles away at Cropston Reservoir to which it runs via Rothley Brook. Since 1997 the reservoir and the surrounding land has been open to the public.

There now follows a real 'basin'. The path is a straight line to the bottom of the hill, through a few trees, and then up the other side, keeping the hedge on your left. On the final corner, you emerge out onto the road at a crossroads. **10**

Cross the road and take the tarmaced Ivanhoe way. (L) After a while the National Forest Way goes straight ahead, but bear right and stay on this tarmaced path now until you reach another tarmaced path which rises on your left **11** . Take this path. After passing through a metal barrier (or gate slightly after barrier) (M), it is not long before you arrive back at the car park on your left.

Route 2 – Mount St. Bernard's Abbey & Whitwick.

Start: The Abbey Car Park (LE67 5UL) – Toilets

Distance: 6.5 miles

Refreshments: St Joseph's Tea Room, Oaks Rd, LE67 5UP

The first Monastery was designed by William Railton (of Nelson's column & Beaumanor Hall fame) and opened in 1837. It was redesigned 7 years later by Augustus Pugin (of Big Ben & Ratcliffe College fame). It became an Abbey in 1848 and Dom Palmer (yes, really!) was the first English Abbot

1 Leave the car park by taking the path in the bottom corner (A).

When this path bends left, turn right and then immediately left to go up to the top corner. The path now goes right, on the other side of the hedge.

When you reach a fork in the path take the right fork (B) and continue with a low wall on your right.

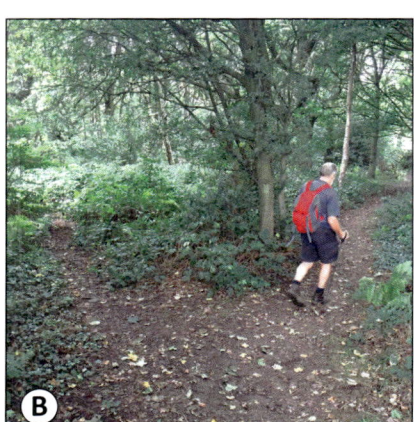

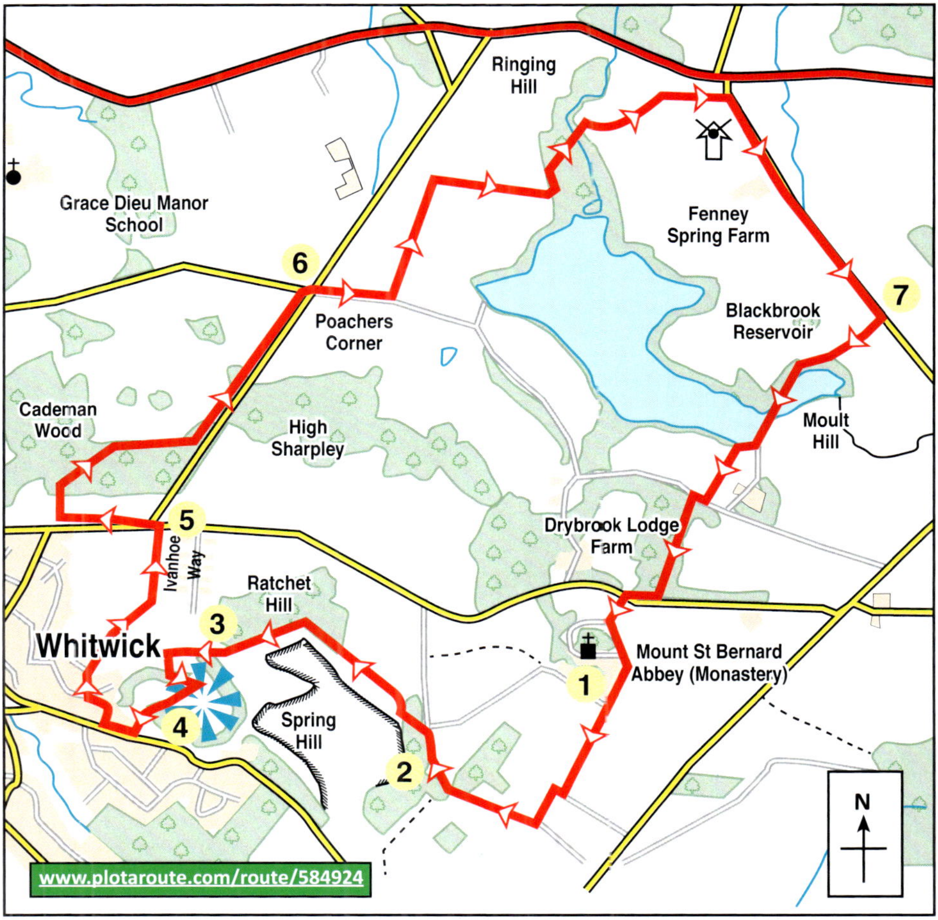
Ringing Hill
Grace Dieu Manor School
Fenney Spring Farm
Blackbrook Reservoir
Poachers Corner
Cademan Wood
High Sharpley
Moult Hill
Drybrook Lodge Farm
Ivanhoe Way
Ratchet Hill
Whitwick
Mount St Bernard Abbey (Monastery)
Spring Hill
N
1
2
3
4
5
6
7
www.plotaroute.com/route/584924

B

Eventually this reaches a track going straight across, turn right here. As you go along you can see on your right the top of the Abbey Tower (C).

C

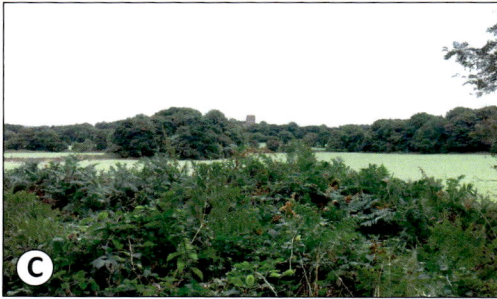

There soon appears to be another fork but the actual path is the left fork (D).

2 You now gradually climb, and looking left through the wire fencing, you can look down into the quarry that has now been filled with water. After a while

you are faced with another fork (E). Either way is alright (the right hand one goes steeply down, the left stays level) as they both merge further on.

Descend this path (F). The rocks on your right are known as Rachet Rocks (G).

Eventually you will see a gate on your left (H) **3**

For a flatter option you can ignore this and continue on and round to the

left and meet the other route at **4**

A more hilly and scenic option is to go through the gate into Forest Rock Wood (I) and start the twisting

path up to the top of the hill. Unfortunately the trees have grown so much now that many of the views

you used to get have been obscured, as has the information board here (J).

Use a path to your right to start the descent but only after about 50 metres you need to look out for a path through the bushes on your right (K), where the obvious path goes straight on.

This path through the bushes eventually reaches a gate which is where you would meet those (coming from the right) who took the flatter option mentioned. Turn left.

4 Keeping the main bushes on your left, continue until you emerge out on to Leicester Road. Turn right along the road and then right into Holgarth Road. Take the footpath on the right next to house No. 18.

This is part of the Ivanhoe way as indicated by the sign post (L). When the path forks, with a large bush in front of you, take the right fork (M).

This soon reaches the brow of the hill and then you descend to the gate in the bottom right hand corner onto a driveway and the Loughborough Road. **5**

(The junction with Swannymore Road is almost opposite, and could be used as a shorter option as it meets up with the longer option at a small car park on the left, continue at **6**)

Turn left and cross over the road. Pass the 'Man within Compass' pub and take the narrow footpath next to house No. 127.

You soon find yourself crossing the pub lawn as you head towards the gap in the stone wall (N). Head half right and slightly up. This part of the route is difficult to describe, but follow the main path and go up a small mound as you pass to the left of a large rock outcrop. This will lead to a small car park on Swannymore Road. Turn left.

6 Take the first lane on your right (opposite Warren Lane). Continue along here until you see a gate in the hedge on your left. The path now goes round the outside of a large field, taking you to a gate in the opposite, diagonal corner. Go through the gate and descend to another gate on your right. This path again descends bringing you out onto a lane and, although not visible here on your right, the northerly tip of Blackbrook Reservoir.

Turn left along the tarmaced Sandhole Lane and then take the footpath on your right (O) which crosses diagonally up the field to reach the same road once more.

Go along by the houses to reach the main Charley Road and turn right. This soon passes the restored Fenney Spring Mill (P). Continue for just over half a mile and then turn right along a Byway (known as One Barrow Lane but not signed such). **7**

This passes Blackbrook Reservoir with extensive views over the reservoir.

The reservoir was constructed in 1796 in order to feed the Charnwood Forest Canal, which has long since vanished. The first dam constructed was an earthworks one, and this failed on 20 February 1799. In eleven minutes the reservoir was empty and as a result local farmland was ruined, sheep were drowned, and much of Shepshed and nearby Loughborough were affected by flood waters. The dam was repaired in 1801, but the canal was no longer commercially viable. The present gravity dam was constructed in 1906. In 1957 the dam felt the effects of a magnitude 5.3 earthquake. The tremors caused heavy coping stones to shift and cracks appeared in the faces of the dam.

At the end of this track you turn right alongside a hedge on your right and then left with a hedge now on your left. Continue up the edge of this field until you reach a track going straight across. Cross this track using the 2 gates. The path now climbs through the trees to reach the Oaks Road. Turn right, cross over the road and into the main entrance to the Abbey and back to the car park.

Route 3 – Barrow, Woodthorpe and Quorn.

Start: Soar Bridge Pub LE12 8PN

Distance: 7.75 miles (Shorter option 6.25 miles)

Refreshments: Soar Bridge in Barrow, Navigation Pub in Barrow & Quorndon Fox pub in Quorn.

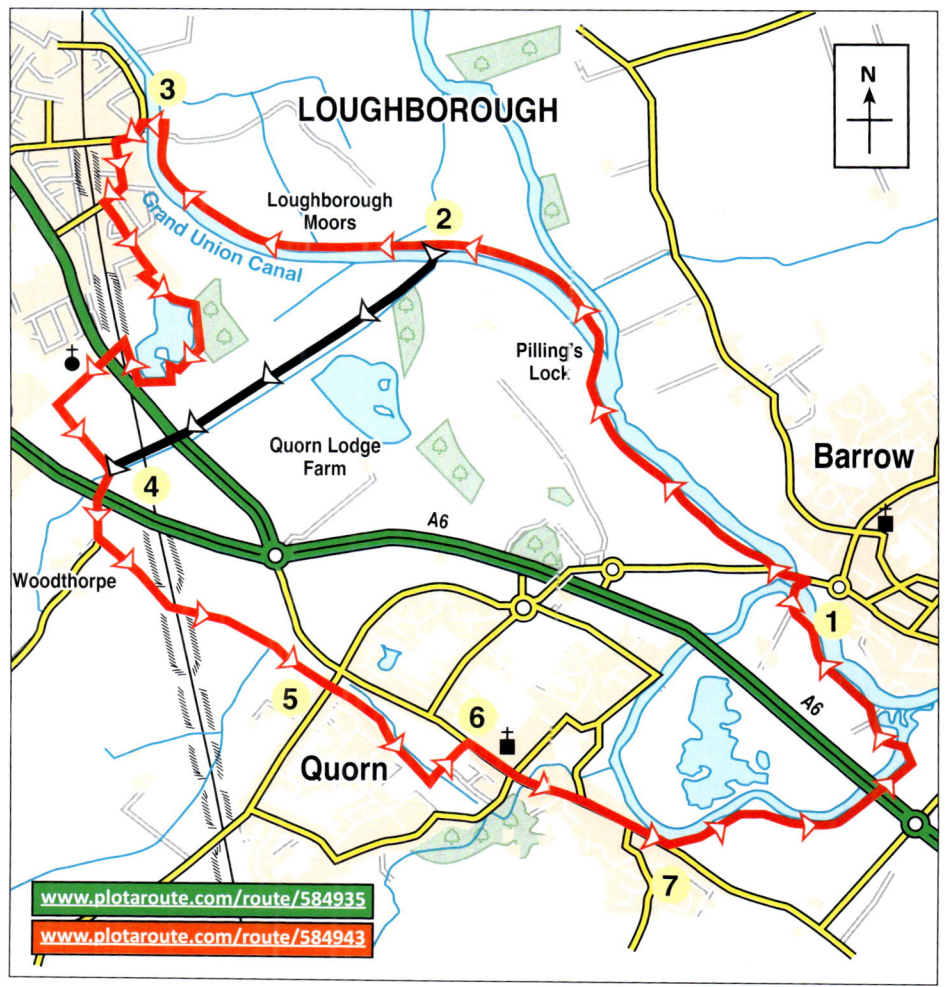

www.plotaroute.com/route/584935
www.plotaroute.com/route/584943

1 Leave the pub car park and go left, cross the road as you approach the bridge over the canal. Immediately after this bridge turn right to pick up the towpath (A). Continue until you reach the bridge over the canal (B) which you need to take so you can go along the other side of the canal. The Pillings Lock Marina & restaurant is visible on your left. Continue to the second bridge (Woodthorpe No. 33). **2**

Shorter route: Go over the stile on the right to take you up onto the bridge. The path continues straight ahead with trees and hedges on your left. Ignore any yellow posts on your left and you eventually come to the main A6 road. Cross over and you go down Lodge End. Continue at **4** below.

Longer route: Continue along the canal towpath until you reach the Moor Lane Bridge No. 35 (C). Take the steps up on your right and go left over the bridge into Moor Lane **3** . Turn left into Great Central Road and then left again into Windmill Road. Your next left turn is into Tuckers Road. Near the bottom of this road you can turn right into a small car park with toilets (D).

Turn left now and you are facing Charnwood Water. Take the path on the left which will lead you clockwise round the water. When you are about three quarters of the way round, look out for a path on your left which leads up and over the railway bridge (E).

The lake called Charnwood Water (formerly Tucker's Pond) was constructed out of the old Tuckers brickworks, which supplied bricks for St. Pancras Station in London. It is the site of the deserted medieval village of Shelthorpe, whose name was used for a 20th century housing estate, situated on the other site of Leicester Road.

You are soon crossing the A6 road and entering the drive to Loughborough Crematorium. Turn left at the end and you eventually leave the grounds into a new housing development. After a short while you reach a path going straight across in front of you, turn right here.

4 Cross over Terry Yardley Way and bear left into Main Street. Just before you reach the houses in Woodthorpe village, take the footpath on the left (F). This crosses the railway line and then over a couple of fields and you reach the Woodhouse Road in Quorn **5** . Cross over, turn right and then take the narrow

footpath on the left (G). This follows the brook on your left until you reach a T junction of paths. Turn left and then you arrive at Sanders Road. Turn left and follow the road round to the right.

This changes into a path which goes down the side of the Quorndon Fox (H) to arrive at High Street (the old A6) **6** . Cross over and turn right. Continue on this road, past the centre of the village (spot island). When the buildings finish and the hedges start on your left, look for and take

the footpath on your left **7** (I).

This path runs alongside the river Soar on your left. Pass under the A6 and after one more field, go through a gate and continue round to the left to cross an old metal bridge and then right along a paved path to reach a lane. Turn right and then left just before crossing the bridge to the Navigation pub (J).

Stay on the canal towpath and you reach a road (K) which, if you turn left, would lead to a caravan park. Our route goes right and you soon reach the pub where you started the route.

Route 4 – Hungarton, Cold Newton, Old Ingarsby, Keyham.

Start: The Black Boy Inn, Hungarton LE7 9JR

Distance: 8.5 miles (shorter option 5 miles)

Refreshments: The Black Boy in Hungarton and The Dog & Gun in Keyham

N.B. The longer option is complex with several gates but is well worth the effort. Just follow the directions a little more carefully.

1 Leave the car park and turn right down Main Street. Take the right-hand bend, then the left bend, but at the next right bend continue ahead into Church Lane (A).

This sweeps round to the left, around the church. Ignore the footpath to the right but instead take the Bridleway through the large metal gate straight ahead. After two more gates, there is a choice of paths. Ignore the one going left but continue ahead and up round the field with the hedge on your left. The next gate is in the left corner (B). The next yellow post is visible straight across the middle of the field (see circle on B) and, at the time of writing, a path had not been left through the crops.

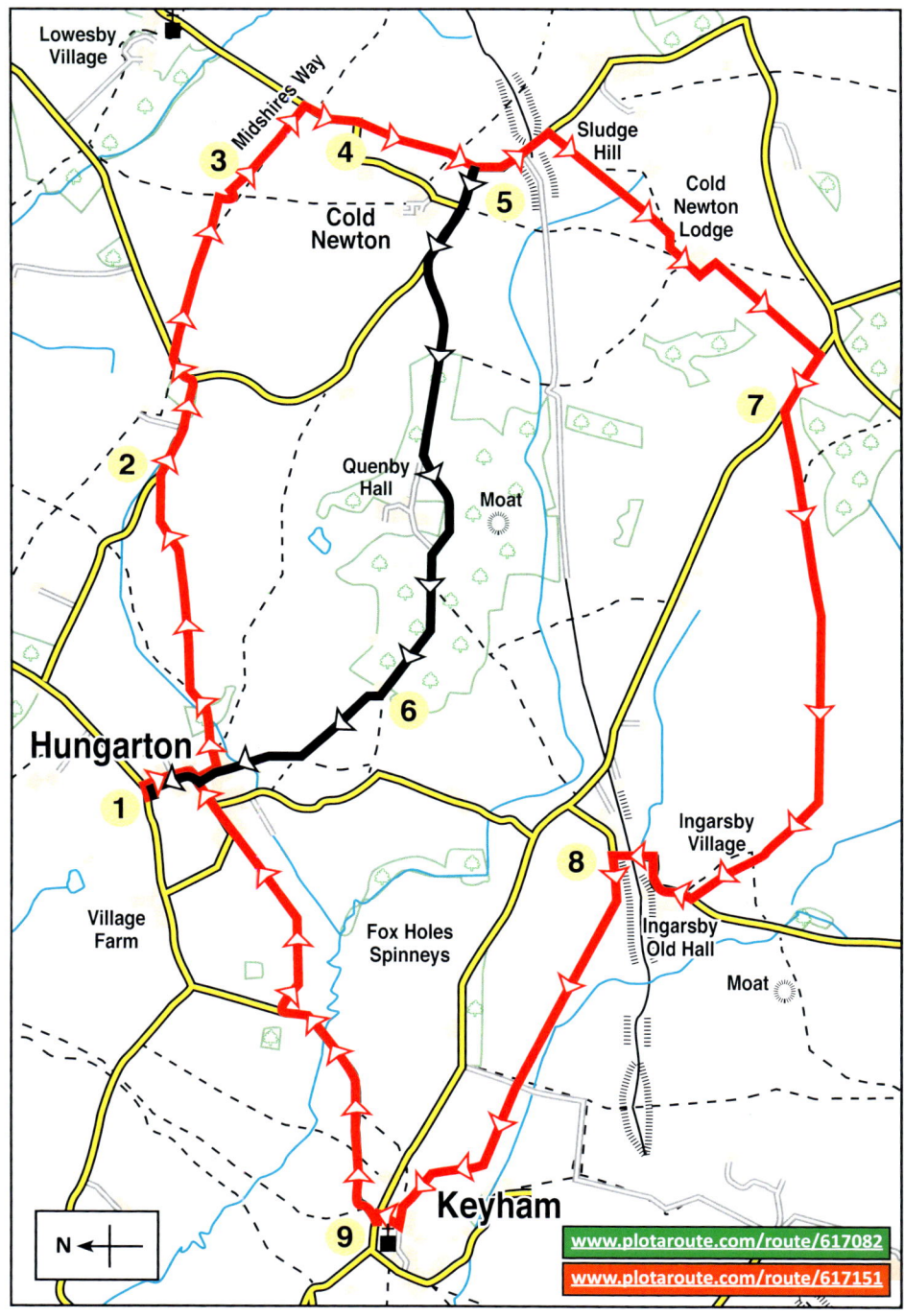

Lowesby
Village

Midshires Way

3

4

Cold
Newton

5

Sludge
Hill

Cold
Newton
Lodge

2

Quenby
Hall

Moat

7

6

Hungarton

1

Ingarsby
Village

8

Village
Farm

Fox Holes
Spinneys

Ingarsby
Old Hall

Moat

9

Keyham

N

(You may wish to go right around the edge of the field fcr easier footing but it is quite a bit further). The following two fields present exactly the same dilemma, but eventually you reach an old wooden gate that leads out onto the road. **2**

Turn right and continue to a T-junction (White's Barn) (C), then go left over the cattle grid. After a small pond on your right, take the bridleway half right across the field (D). This is the Midshires

Way to Cold Newton. It is a slight descent to the metal gate and yellow post.

The route across the next field is not obvious, but continue straight ahead and once you cross the brow the yellow post and gate can be seen down in the bushes (E). A short, steep climb now awaits you. Keep the hedges on your right and

eventually descend to the yellow post and gate in the bottom corner (F). The yellow posts can be a little confusing here because you have just reached another footpath going straight across in front of you, especially as you need to go right for a few metres to the next post then go left over a stony bridge over a ditch (G) **3** .

The path you don't want goes r ght to another post and stile into an area of trees. However, your path still goes right, but keeps to the left of the fenced tree area (just behind top of yellow post in G) and then to a gate straight ahead.

Although the obvious path continues ahead, with the stream over to your right (which you can do and then swing left at the fence head), the actual path goes diagonally left and up to a gate in the opposite top corner of the field.

Through this gate you reach a tarmaced road (H) **4** . The Midshires Way goes stra ght ahead here, but you go right, along the road towards Cold Newton. Just as the road bends right, continue straight on to a small gate and yellow post between a fence and hedge (I). Continue over the field, keeping the hedge

on your right, and an old, small gate in the bottom corner takes you out on to the road **5** . (A sighting of Billesdor Coplow comes into view ahead).

Shorter Option: Turn right along the road. Ignore the footpath on the left opposite the road up to into Cold Newton village. At the top of the hill, turn left through a large wooden

gate (painted red with a white top bar) (J). You are now on the track leading to Quenby Hall. As the Hall gets nearer and you reach a fence on your right, bear half left over the field (K), the next yellow post is on

the corner of the wall round the grounds (see

circle on K). Go alongside the wall and notice that the ground to your right is level with the top of the wall.

This feature is called a Ha-Ha and is thought to have originated in France. As one approached the wall from the upper level and then suddenly realised there was a drop down, the exclamation of surprise - Ah Ah! -would be heard.

Go through the gate at the end of the wall and bear half right to reach the main drive of the hall.

Quenby Hall is a Jacobean house which has been described as the most important early seventeenth century house in Leicestershire (now grade 1 listed). The Hall was built between 1618 and 1636 by George Ashby and remained in the Ashby family until 1904. (L)

Continue down the drive, ignoring a yellow post and path going off diagonally left, to reach a cattle grid between two stone pillars **6** (M). Take the small stile on your right and proceed down the edge of the field. You could continue to the bottom and then bear left keeping the hedge on your

right, but sometimes there is a tractor track going half left which

cuts the corner, but both options take you to a yellow post and a railed wooden bridge in the hedge.

Up and over the next field to drop down to the gate, a bridge and then two more small gates (N). You now come out on Church Lane where you started. Turn right at junction with Main Street to get back to the Black Boy Inn.

Longer option: Turn left at the road. After crossing a disused railway cutting, take the bridleway on your right towards Cold Newton Lodge. According to maps, it appears that the footpath used to swing left towards the lodge and then right again later, but now they want you to continue on a line straight ahead. Just before you get to the next building, take the small gate in the hedge on your right, and then go left, so the

hedge now is on your left. As you reach the drive to this house, you will see a yellow post giving you a choice of right or straight on, you go straight on. Be somewhat cautious now, as there are yellow posts scattered all over, some of which do not seem to be on the OS maps at the time of writing. When the fenced-in trees of the garden end, on your left, swing round to the left (O) towards the yellow post in the

hedge, which takes you out onto the driveway for the house. Turn right and continue down to the road, then turn right. Look out now for a large and small metal gate on the left (P) **7** . There is no footpath sign here because this path is known as a Public Access Route. Taking this path gradually takes you away from the line of the road you were on and, although quite clear at the start, gets rather lacking in yellow posts.

Eventually you will bear right and go down to a stile in the hedge, just before the bottom corner (circled on Q). This takes you to a narrow path between bushes before

reaching an open field which ascends slightly. Keep the hedge on your right to the next gate. Be careful here because the first arrow/post you see would take you over to the left, but a little further on, in the hedge, is one showing you that you can go straight on and head for the house in the distance, which is Ingarsby Old Hall (R).

Ingarsby Old Hall, built by Sir Brian Cave, was originally moated on three sides. The oldest parts date to the 1540s with further additions in around 1621. Ingarsby is a deserted medieval village, which is now protected as a scheduled monument. It is thought to have been established during the 9th or 10th century, and by 1086 is recorded as having 32 heads of households in the Doomesday Book. It was deserted in 1469 and the land used for pasture. You can still see mounds where the houses used to be and hollows where the streets were.

The path reaches the road in front of Ingarsby Old Hall. Turn right and stay on the road until you have passed under a large railway arch and then take the footpath on the left (S) **8** .

Ignore the yellow post you may be able to see over on the right, but instead, keeping the hedge on your left, look out for a yellow post in the hedge (see circle on S.) which leads down some steps to a narrow bridge over the stream. Go up the other side and turn right (see circle on T) and keep the hedges on your right (even though an arrow on the post says bear left to another yellow post in the bushes above you).

Through a narrow gap in the fencing (blue arrow) keep a look out for where the path goes right, through the hedge and across a bridge (U). Up the bank on the other side and turn left, keep the hedges and brook on your left. At the end of the field the path swings right, to climb the side of the field, BUT you need to look out for a very narrow hole in the hedge (V) and a yellow post to pass through into the next field. Once again, it is along the bottom of the field with hedges on your left.

A yellow post indicates where you get through the next hedge as it takes you down a few steps and a stile with the brook now close on your left. Along the bottom of the field once more, this time the yellow post is visible just up along the hedge in front of you. Here there is a gate with a stile over the fence into a small field before the next stile which leads into the Four Seasons Nature Reserve. On leaving this area, the next yellow post can be seen to the right of a large, low shed; as can the next one a little further on.

After these, the path goes half right across the front of some property and into another field. Again half right over and up this field to a yellow post along the top. Turn half left and go across the field (see circle on W). There is now a narrow path between garden fences, which brings you out on the road in Keyham (X). Take the next right

(Kings Lane) to the junction with Ingarsby Road.

Go left here (Y) and cross over into Hungarton Lane 9 . Continue down the hill, passing two footpath signs on your right. After the left-hand bend, the road starts to climb. Just when you think you have a long hill to get up, a footpath sign on your right showing 'Hungarton Road half a mile' comes to your rescue. So it is into the fields again, keeping hedges on your left. After the next metal gate, I found moving out into the field

a little made it easier going underfoot. From the next gate you can see the path in front of you heading for the houses of Hungarton (Z). At the road (Coal Baulk) it is a right turn to the junction and then left up the hill back to the Black Boy pub.

Route 5 – Birstall, Watermead & Abbey Park – A flat route by rivers and canals.

Start: White Horse Pub, White Horse Lane, Birstall LE4 4EF

Distance: 7.75 miles (shorter 6 mile option)

Refreshments: The White Horse pub and Peppercorns Café in Abbey Park

1 Turn right out of the car park then go right again over the bridge with white railings (A). Follow the towpath and then turn left over the next bridge.

Turn immediately right so you have the canal on your right and the river on your left. Cross the long concrete bridge (B).

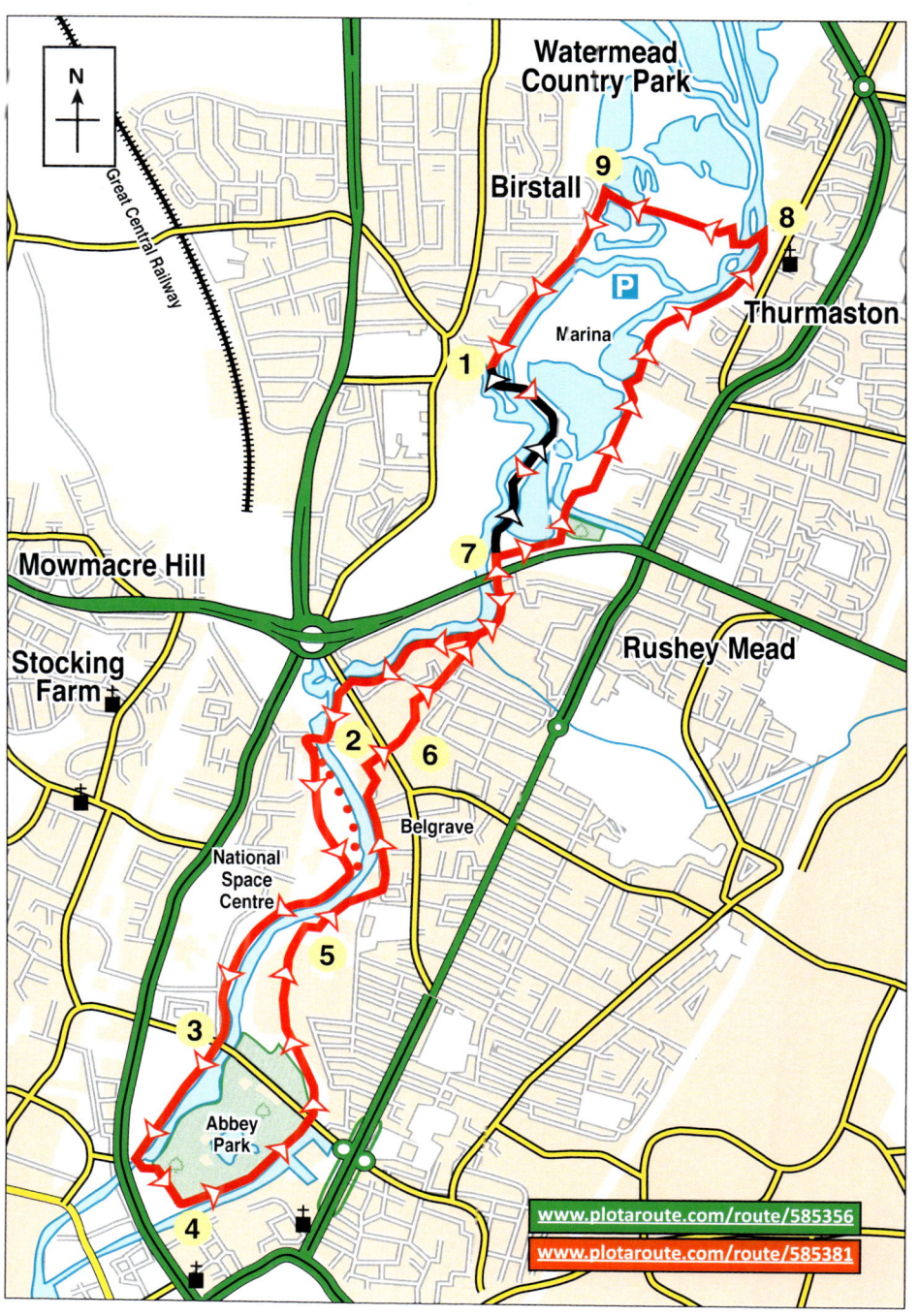

N

Watermead
Country Park

Birstall

9

8

Thurmaston

P

Marina

1

7

Mowmacre Hill

Rushey Mead

Stocking
Farm

2

6

Belgrave

National
Space
Centre

5

3

Abbey
Park

4

Great Central Railway

Go past canal lock No 45 and continue along here until it eventually takes you under the road (Watermead Way) (C). Take the right hand track rather than the tarmaced path to avoid any cyclists. After crossing a small, concrete sided bridge, keep right to pass over a railed bridge. Take the next right fork, keeping the river on your right and follow the path going under the bridge for Loughborough Road (D)

(NB. A new path is being created here on your left but not sure when it will be open).

At the next bridge take the left fork up onto Thurcaston Road. **2** Cross over the road and head right, over the river bridge, then take the footpath on the left towards Abbey Park.

Take the right fork, signed Ellis Meadows (E) (you could go straight ahead, keeping the river on your left, and end up at the same place). Use the left fork and lower path to reach a T junction where you turn right, and then left over a wooden bridge. The path leads you past the National Space Centre (F).

Ignoring the large bridge to your left and footpaths to the right, you reach Abbey Park Road **3** . Use the pedestrian crossing to go over the road and enter Abbey Park. Keep straight ahead, with water on your left (G), and pass by the recently refurbished Pavilion Cafe (Peppercorns) on your right (good cakes!) (H).

Abbey Park, with its bandstand, rustic bridges and planted gardens, was the work of William Barron, a celebrated landscape designer. It was Leicester's first public park of significant size, and was opened on 29 May 1882 by the Prince and Princess of Wales.

Ignore the large stone bridge on your left and instead, go straight ahead. Leave the park, by going through a gate in the wall and then turn left over a concrete bridge (St Margaret's Way can be seen over on the right). Turn left then right and continue with all-weather courts on your right to the end of the path where you cross the car park area and take the steps down to the canal **4** and turn left again to take the towpath.

At the fork in the towpath keep right, going under Abbey Park Road. When you reach the next bridge, bear right so that you can cross it,

5 (I) then turn left passing a lock (J). Ignore the large bridge on the left but instead turn

right towards the road (Ross Walk).

After carefully missing the concrete bollards, turn left along the path. You now have the river on your left and the backs of a row of houses on your right. Continue into the 'No Through Road' but look out for the left fork into Belgrave Gardens. Take this and then fork right to go by the side of Belgrave House. Exit the gardens by passing through the large wrought iron gates (K). Belgrave Hall and Gardens are opposite.

Belgrave Hall is a Queen Anne-style Grade II listed building with walled gardens. It was built as a family home for Edmund and Ann Cradock in 1709. (At this time, Belgrave was a small village, 3 miles from Leicester). After only 2 years from its completion, both had died, and it was then owned by the Simons family for 45 years, the Vann family for 78 years, (during which time they also built the nearby Belgrave House), the Ellis family for 76 years, and Thomas Morley for 13 years. In 1936 it was bought by Leicester City Council, at which point it became a museum. Recently, the Council made the decision to use the house and gardens as a heritage site rather than a museum, and it is now only open at certain times during the summer months. It is also available for private functions, such as weddings and ghost watches.

Turn left to the T junction where the Talbot Pub is on the corner, then right into Thurcaston Road. Go straight over the traffic lights into Bath St. **6** . Look out for the house on your right (L).

This house, known as the Belgrave Adult School was opened by the Ellis family in 1847. It was used to teach reading and writing to adults (6am start !) and it was one of the first establishments for adult education outside of a major town.

Follow the road as it bends round to the left and turn right through the concrete bollards (M). Where the road bends right, go left on a footpath, then keep to the right of a large gated entrance (marked Route 6). Go right at the junction of paths to go over the railed bridge and follow the path you were on earlier. Now over the concrete bridge and take the left fork to go under the road once more. **7**

Shorter route: Go straight ahead on the same path you came out on, past the lock and back to the pub.

Longer route: Ignore the first small path on the right, as this only leads up to the road above, but take the next tarmaced path to the right. The path eventually swings left. After crossing a wooden section of path (actually a bridge), leave the main path by ascending the steps on your right. Be prepared for the Woolly Mammoth at the top! (N) Spare a moment to take in the views (O) and then head down the grass path towards the. car park. Stay on the tarmaced path between the lake and the car park. This then changes to a gravel path.

At the end, swing left to have a steel fence and building on your right. Where this fence ends, turn right (P) to get a fence on both sides and a Marina on your left. This path eventually opens out onto a large grassed area - head towards the buildings on your right by taking the left hand path by the river and then swing left round behind some trees to a narrow gate. After three more narrow gateways you reach a small car park and Thurmaston Boatyard. **8**

The house opposite was once a pub (The True Blue) and the faded bricks at the front left hand side of the building clearly show where the pub sign used to be.

Turn left over 2 bridges, then right and left again over a third bridge (Q). Continue straight ahead and you will soon see lakes on either side of the path. At signpost 48 **9** turn left to Whiles Lane (R).

Where there are forks in the path, go left twice to stay on Route 48. Squeeze through the metal plates to leave the Country Park, and then follow the path by the water back to the pub, on your right.

Route 6 – Ratby, Groby Pool & Martinshaw Woods.

Start: The Plough Inn, Burroughs Rd, Ratby, LE6 0XZ

Distance: 7m (Shorter option 5m)

Refreshments: The Plough Inn

1 Walk down the slope out of the car park and turn right along the tarmaced lane. Ignore the first footpath sign on your right which cuts back over to the houses, but instead, take the next footpath on the

right which takes you gradually away from the lane (A) and into the bushes. Follow the yellow posts through here (B), being aware later of tree roots under foot in places.

You eventually emerge on to a gravel track **2** where you need to turn right to get to a drive with a house on your left. Immediately opposite you should see a yellow post (C), directing you into an open field. Take this and keep the hedges on your left as you first ascend the small hill and then descend to the post in the far corner, which then comes out onto Markfield Road.

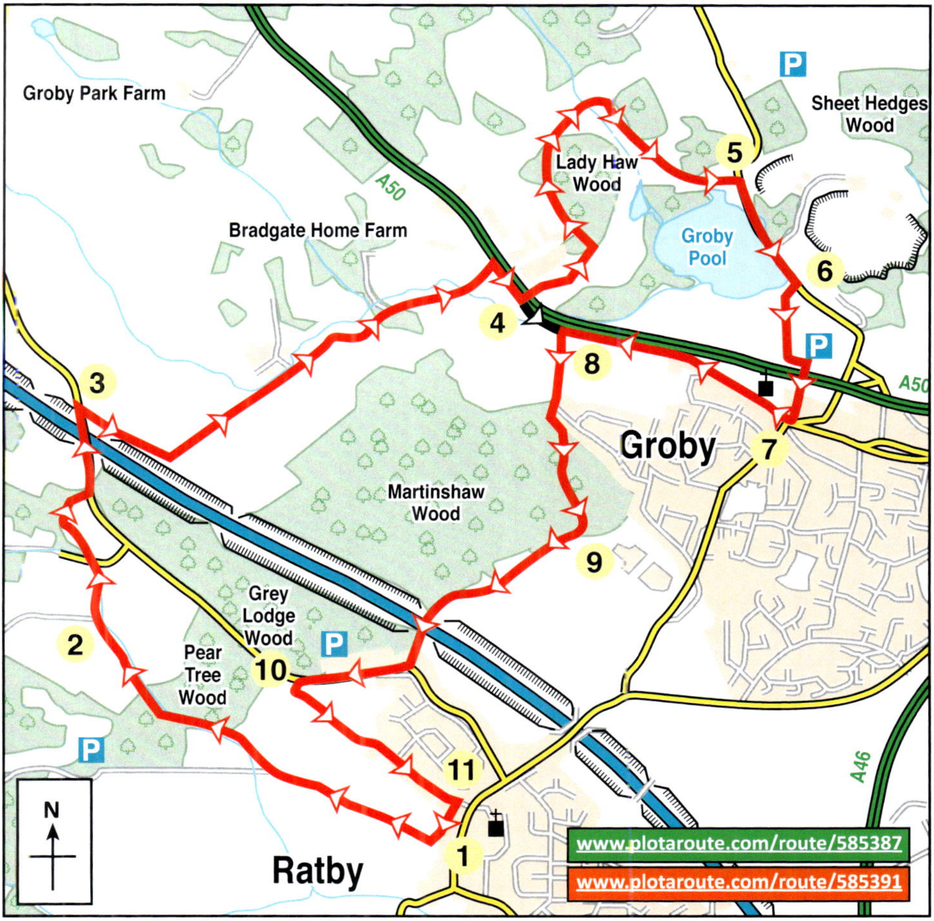

Map labels:

Groby Park Farm

Sheet Hedges Wood

Lady Haw Wood

5

Bradgate Home Farm

Groby Pool

6

4

8

3

Groby

7

Martinshaw Wood

9

Grey Lodge Wood

2

Pear Tree Wood

10

A50

A46

11

N

1

Ratby

www.plotaroute.com/route/585387

www.plotaroute.com/route/585391

Turn left and cross over the road and you are soon passing under the M1 motorway. Where there is a driveway on the right, look for the footpath sign on the right which directs you to double back on yourself between hedges (D) **3** .

At the bottom of the path, you are directed left across fields, keeping the hedge on your left. This will lead on to a tarmaced driveway passing several farm buildings and a lake. From here, all the way down to the main A50, the drive is lined with rhododendrons, which, if at the right time of the year, are quite spectacular. Turn right along the pavement. **4**

Shorter route: Continue until the road starts to sweep to the left and then look for the public footpath sign on the right marked National Forest Way, which will lead you into Martinshaw Woods (K). Continue at **8** below.

Longer route: Carefully cross over the dual carriageway and look for the footpath sign

leading up a wide track (E). The path veers to the left at a large metal gate, but is clearly signed (F). When a footpath seems to continue straight ahead, make sure that you veer left, so that the garden

fences stay close on your left hand side.

There is a stile to climb over and then a gate leads you into an open field. There are now 2 obvious paths in front of you (G). The one that goes right, down the side of the field, is the preferable one, but if at all wet under foot, it's best to avoid this one as it gets quite boggy at the bottom of the slope. In which case, take the path straight ahead which will lead to another metal swing gate, and then bear right over to a yellow post on the main

track going straight across. Whichever path you have taken, turn right when you reach the main track. This eventually reaches a road **5** .

Turn right at the road, there is a path you can take which is safer than being on the road (H). This passes along the shore of Groby Pool. There is one short section where you need to go on the road but you can soon get back on to the footpath. Go down a few concrete steps at the side of a bench seat which overlooks the lake.

Groby Pool is the largest natural lake in the county, covering 38 acres. Although Groby village is noted in the Domesday Book, there is no mention of a lake. The earliest recorded reference is dated 1297, which refers to two pools in Groby.

When you reach the private drive to Pool House, turn into it **6** but take the footpath just inside on the left (I).

The path now crosses the middle of a field and heads for Groby Church (which, at time of writing, is just visible over the tops of the trees).

On the far side of the field, go through a metal gate in the hedge and then turn left. You soon swing right and pass under the A50 road and then go up alongside the church

on your left (J) to reach Markfield Road, **7** where you must turn right. At the A50 turn left and continue down

to the bend in the road, and then look for the public footpath sign on the left, marked National Forest Way, which will lead you into Martinshaw Woods (K).

8 Here the path goes slightly up and eventually swings right to a boarded bridge over a ditch and then a metal gate into the woods proper. Keep left where the path joins

another path coming from the right (L). Where the path swings right, go straight across another track by crossing

the 2 boarded bridges over ditches (M). The path now continues ahead through the trees until you reach a hedge in front of you, this is where you need to turn right. You

should see a school playground on your left.

A little further on, go through a metal gate that leads into an open field **9** (N). The path is quite clear here and you pass Martinshaw Lodge on your right before coming out on a track which crosses the M1, and then leads to Markfield Lane.

Martinshaw Wood can be traced back to at least the 13th century and covers 254 acres. Martinshaw Lodge was also known as the Woodkeeper's Cottage.

Turn right and keep within the slip road for the houses along here on your right to stay safe. Where the houses end, and at the bend in the main road, cross over and take care not to miss the footpath sign which is almost hidden in the hedge **10** (O). After a short hedge lined path, you bear left and head for where

the narrow path runs between two fences. This leads into the end

of Stamford Street. Go along this street, looking for the second footpath on your right (P), called The Stattie. Turning right here will lead you back to the pub car park.

Route 7 – Newtown Linford, Ulverscroft and Copt Oak.

Start: The Bradgate Pub, Newtown Linford, LE6 0AE

Distance: 7miles (shorter option 5 miles)

Refreshments: The Bradgate Pub,

1 Turn right out of the pub car park. Ignore Markfield Lane on the left, but cross over and shortly take the footpath on the left between two houses (A). Go over a couple of fields until you cross a narrow bridge into Bailey Sim wood (B).

The footpath goes straight across here, you need to go left but only for a few yards, when you need to turn right off this main path and climb up past the derelict Ulverscroft Watermill (C) on your right.

This listed building was built in the early 19th century and was a corn mill. The original grinding stones remain on site.

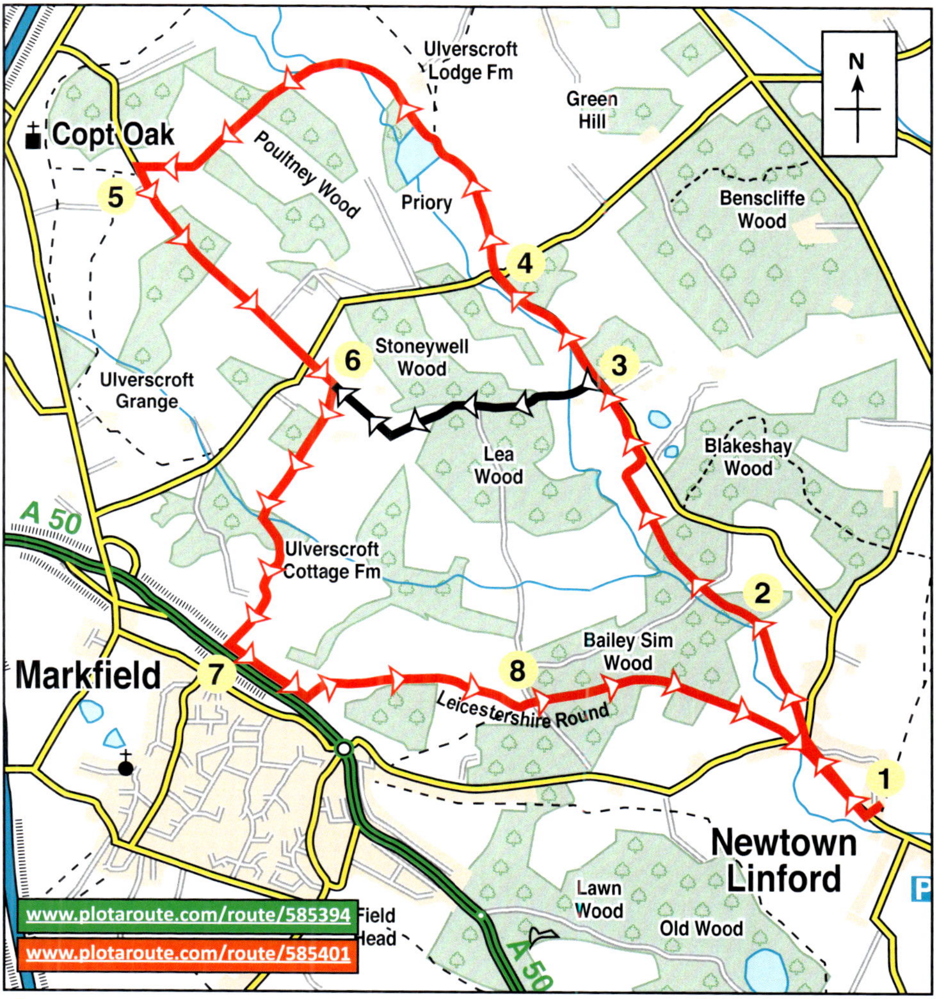

Map labels:
- Ulverscroft Lodge Fm
- Green Hill
- Copt Oak
- **5**
- Poultney Wood
- Priory
- Benscliffe Wood
- **4**
- Stoneywell Wood
- **6**
- **3**
- Ulverscroft Grange
- Lea Wood
- Blakeshay Wood
- A 50
- Ulverscroft Cottage Fm
- **2**
- Markfield
- **7**
- Bailey Sim Wood
- **8**
- Leicestershire Round
- **1**
- Newtown Linford
- Lawn Wood
- Old Wood
- Field Head
- www.plotaroute.com/route/585394
- www.plotaroute.com/route/585401
- A 50
- N

2 Continue straight ahead now, crossing a track which leads to a small fishing lake on your left. When you emerge from the wood into a field, go straight ahead across the middle of the field. At the end, in the trees, ignore the gate on your left which could lead you round a Site of Special Scientific Interest, but instead turn right up to the road which is Ulverscroft Lane. Go left along the road to where Polly Botts Lane goes to the left **3** .

Shorter route - Turn left up Polly Botts Lane, a steady climb, with a right hand bend near the top where it changes to Lea Lane. On your right is the National Trust site of Stoneywell Cottage. A little further on is a wooden roadside seat on your right. Your footpath is just here on the left (G). Continue at **6** below.

Longer route - Continue along Ulverscroft Lane to reach the junction at Priory Lane **4** .

Go straight across onto the tarmac footpath. Very soon you are passing by the ruins of Ulverscroft Priory (D).

Founded in 1139 by Robert de Beaumont, second Earl of Leicester, it was originally built of wood and became an Augustinian Priory later that century. After it was dissolved in the 16th century, it had various owners, those of the Ferrers, Grey and Manners family. It gradually became a ruin and the Priory door was used as the main door to Thornton Church. In 1927, Sir William Everard (of Ratcliffe Hall) bought the premises with a view to preserving the decaying ruins from total destruction.

You eventually reach a large wooden gate across the drive. Go through the small gate on the right of it (E), then cross the drive to a second small gate. The path now crosses half right over a grassy field to reach a stile & yellow post. Continue ahead with the wood on your left and just before the end of

the field turn left, over a small bridge into the trees (F).

Your route basically stays straight ahead, even though you cross a couple of well-established tracks. The last climb up, with a wood on your left, bears slightly right towards the top to reach the road by farm buildings **5** . (This is Whitcrofts Lane, and the Copt Oak Inn could be reached by taking the footpath opposite).

Turn left here and continue for a longish stretch on this road to the junction with Priory Lane once more. (The car park on your right, just before the junction, is used by visitors to the NT site of Stoneywell Cottage).

Go straight across into Lea Lane, and you will soon see a wooden, roadside seat on your left. Turn right here on to the footpath (G).

Stoneywell Cottage on Lea Lane was designed by Ernest Gimson (1864-1919) in the 'Arts & Crafts' style (he was a leading light of the movement which he started in 1880), and built in 1899. The roof, like many of Gimson's houses, was originally thatch, but following a fire in 1938 was re-roofed in second-hand Swithland slates. It remained in the family until 2012 when the National Trust took it over. At present, it is open to the public on Mondays but visits must be booked in advance.

6 The path gradually descends, crossing a wide farm track on the way, and passing through several tree lined avenues, making this one of the more picturesque parts of the route. Eventually a set of well-spaced steps lead to a gate **7** . Straight ahead is a concrete subway under the A50 (H), but ignore this and instead head left through the gap in the fence, again through the trees. You will reach a place on your left where there is a yellow post directing you straight ahead and a concrete manhole. Go left here through the fence (missing stile at time of writing) into a field of (possible) long grass and young trees. This path is not marked as such but is obvious and leads to another stile.

Go over this stile and then left downhill, looking for a gate in the hedge on your right leading into open fields. The route now heads diagonally left and slightly up (I). At the top go left and eventually you go through a gate in the hedge on your right. There are usually horses in these next fields but the path is fenced off as you proceed along the left hand side. After the last gate, the path crosses diagonally

right to the farmhouse, and then left to join a main track. **8** (J) John's Lea Wood is to the left. Go straight across and through a gate, back into Bailey Sim Wood. (Through the trees on your left, you may spot a tower used for abseiling by various outdoor pursuits groups).

Another bush/tree lined track to go along (ignoring the yellow posted route on a fork to the left) and when this runs out, turn right through the metal gate in the hedge. Turn left along the hedge to another gate and then diagonally right across the next field (K) to come out on the road at the bottom of Markfield Lane. Go left for a short way and then right. Cross over and back to the Bradgate Pub.

Route 8 – Saxelbye, Grimston, Old Dalby & Wartnaby.

Start: Main St, Saxelbye LE14 3PQ

(You may have been here before when doing Route 9 in Volume 1, but this is a loop north of Saxelbye. Webster's Dairy on Main Street was founded in 1883, and is one of only six dairies where Stilton Cheese is manufactured.)

Distance: 7.5 miles (shorter option 5.5 miles)

Refreshments: The Black Horse pub in Grimston

1 Go west along Main St and under the railway bridge to the junction which is Saxelbye Lane. The footpath is via a style in the hedge opposite. Go right for a few metres, then left and up to the next yellow post. Take the path up the right hand side of the hedge. Eventually at a yellow post where there is a large gap in the hedge, turn right and cross the open field. After the next field you reach a tarmac road **2** (A). Ignore the path going straight across and instead go left over the cattle grid. The house and garden on your right is Saxelbye Park.

Saxelbye Park is the seat of the Wright family, who own most of the Saxelbye estate.

Although there are also paths on the right, these are usually over ploughed fields, so stay on this road to the junction and then turn right. The road first winds left then right. Take the footpath on the right, just where the hedge finishes **3** (B). Keeping next to the hedge, the path stays on the left bank of the brook all the way into Grimston (C).

Grimston was once a railway station serving Saxelbye village

As you turn right on the road, note the ancient stocks on the green. At the junction **4** you can see the Black Horse pub across the green in front of you.

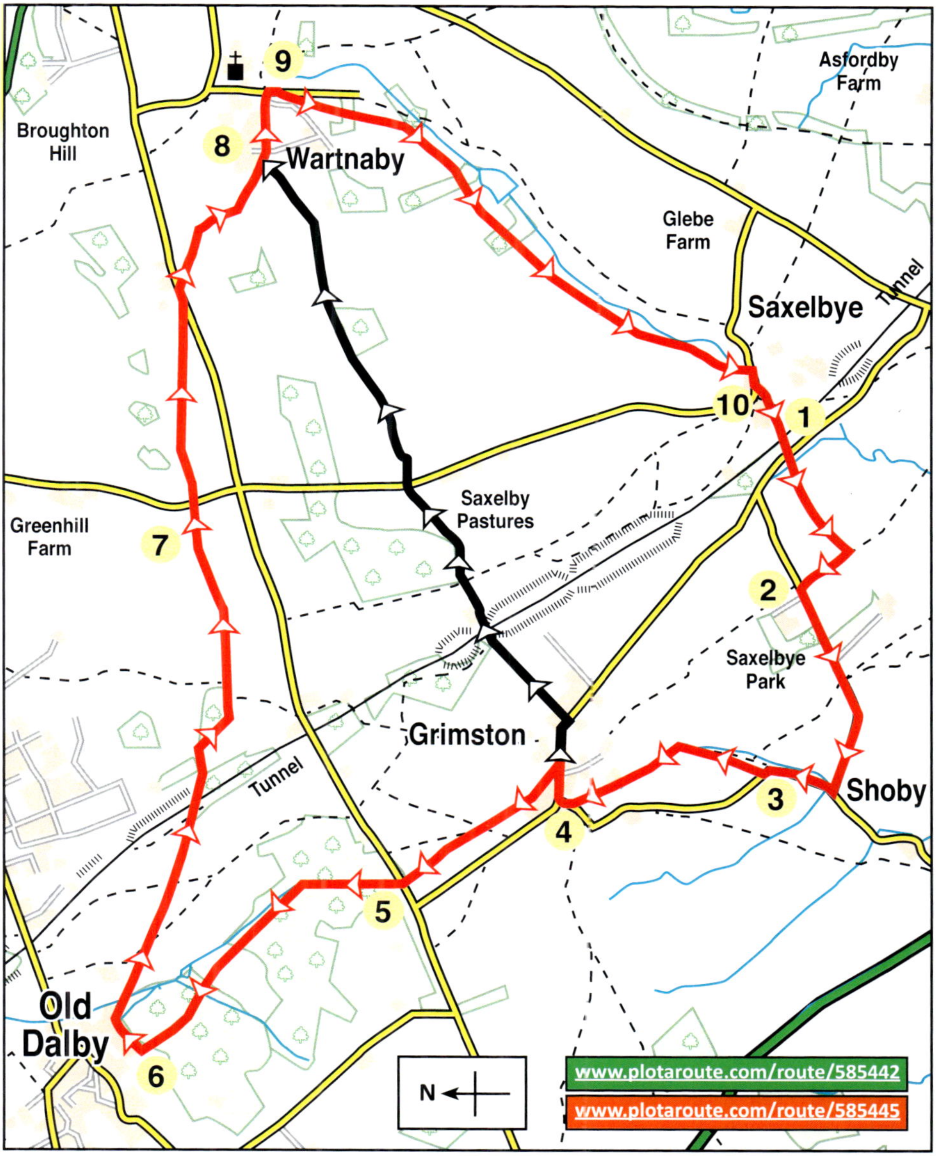

Broughton Hill

Asfordby Farm

9

8 **Wartnaby**

Glebe Farm

Tunnel

Saxelbye

10 **1**

Greenhill Farm

7

Saxelby Pastures

2

Saxelbye Park

Grimston

3 **Shoby**

4

Tunnel

5

Old Dalby

6

N ←

www.plotaroute.com/route/585442

www.plotaroute.com/route/585445

Shorter option: Turn right and go through the village. Not long after the road swings to the right, take footpath on the left which goes up through Lilac Farm (D). After the second metal gate, the path goes left and then right to go around the horse field.

D

As you ascend this path, you are not aware that you are passing over a railway line which passes through the hill at this point.

The railway line opened in 1880. It was once part of the London, Nottingham main line until it closed in 1968. It now forms part of the Old Dalby Test Track.

After crossing the road, the path is now a wide track all the way to the village of Wartnaby.

Continue at **8** below.

Longer Route: Turn right, but look on your left for some concrete steps going up between two houses. (The footpath sign is on the right hand side of the road). Follow

the path between the garden fences to emerge into an open field (E). Across the field you reach a couple of stiles together. Cross the field to the top left corner. Here there is a choice of three paths, two straight ahead but the one

you want is accessed by going through the metal gate on the left and then turning right to have the hedge on your right. At the

end of this field the yellow post is over to the left slightly. This stile takes you out onto the road, which you then cross and enter Old Dalby Wood **5** (F).

This is a wide vehicular track which descends through the trees, but look out for the yellow post on your right where the public footpath forks away (G). Strangely,

this eventually reaches the vehicle track further down and you turn right on it to continue. However, it is not long

before you need to fork right again at a yellow post as the track straight on is a private road (H).

You descend again to a plank bridge and then up the bank the other side. You leave the wood by crossing a second plank bridge and continue straight ahead (between the crops if it is that time of year) (I).

Over the field to a stile and a few more trees. The path over the next field starts by going over a brow and then you can see a large tree which you pass to the right of, and then slightly veer right, passing a low wall to the left (the grounds

of Old Dalby Hall) and then the yellow post is visible in the distance (see circle on J), which takes you out onto the road in the village of Old Dalby **6**

Turn right along the road and proceed to where the road bends left, here you take the footpath on your right, then a wooden gate, back into the trees. Cross the plank bridge at the top into a field. Keep the hedge on your right, to the end of the field and then swing left and you are able to see the next yellow post in the hedge on your right. Through here and then turn left round the edge of the field. Go right at the bottom and the next yellow post is halfway along on your left. There is a main track going across your route here, but cross this and use the stile opposite (K).

The footpath here is half right but if there are crops you will need to stay right parallel to the main track on the other side of the hedge and then left at the end to reach the yellow

post and stile up on your right. The path continues diagonally over the next field. Once over the brow, you can see the next yellow post which leads you into a small wood. Bear slightly left over the old railway and head down

through the trees to the stile at the bottom (L) and then half right to the next yellow post. Spot the large lake over to your left and then a smaller, pretty lake on the right which you pass clockwise around, to reach a wide plank bridge and head left, keeping the spinney on the left.

There is quite a good climb here to the next yellow post near the trees and then continue to another stile into some more trees. After a short distance you are presented with a choice of paths (M) and you need to go right, through a Conservation area of young trees. You come out of the woods by crossing over a stile. At this point the path stays in a straight line with hedges on your left and the road over to the right.

You need to cross a minor road **7** and take the path opposite. There's now another long field, keeping to the left of it. Over a stile, and a slight swerve right here so that you once again have the hedges on your left. Look out for one of the yellow posts which points half right taking you diagonally over the field to a footpath sign just protruding above the hedge next to the main road (not the metal barred gate). Cross the road and go left to the next wide gated entrance to a field (for tractors etc) and the yellow

post is half right in the hedge in front of you (N). (The actual footpath sign to leave the road is just past this entrance if the gate is closed). A couple of large fields to cross now (see circle on N), all well marked, and you eventually reach a wide, definite track running across right to left in front of you. Turn left here into the village of Wartnaby (O).

8 On reaching the village (O), head in an easterly direction.

Wartnaby was once the property of the Knights Templar, now partially owned and managed by the Friars Wells Estate. Friars Wells was originally the Vicarage, then purchased by Colonel John Dane Player (of Players cigarettes), who was killed in action in 1943. The name is probably derived from the Old English for "Watch Tower", a look-out post. Tower Cottage at the eastern end of the village is dated 1656 and has this unusual water tower on the roof (hence its name). Adjacent are the remains of a 12th or 13th Century building possibly connected with the Knights Templar.

A strange aspect here is that there is a black wooden gate across the road . There is also

a smaller pedestrian gate on the left of the larger gate which can be opened by pressing the rocker switch mounted on a post just before it. The gate will automatically close itself. A little further on, the road swings left, but you need to turn right, however, be careful because your footpath is now immediately on your right **9** (P).

As you cross the right hand side of this field you pass the gardens of Wartnaby Hall on your right.

Wartnaby Hall is set in magnificent and well landscaped gardens. It is said that King Charles II took breakfast here. It was occupied by military forces during the second world war. (Up for sale recently at £800K)

Head across the field towards a small copse and then veer right to continue with the brook on your left. After approximately a mile you reach the road in Saxelbye **10** (Q). Turn right through the village back to the starting point.

Route 9 – Gaddesby, Ashby Folville, Thorpe Satchville & Barsby.

Start: The Cheney Arms, Gaddesby LE7 4XE

Distance: 8.75 miles (shorter options of 4.5 [1,2,3,7,8,1] or 4.25 miles [3,4,5,6,4,3])

Refreshments: Cheney Arms (Gaddesby) and Carington Arms (Ashby Folville)

![Cheney Arms pub exterior]

1 Leave the pub car park and turn right and then immediately right again into Chapel Lane (A). Continue to the top of the lane and where it swings left into the drive for Firs Farm, go right at the fork (B) to pass alongside the lawned garden to reach a metal swing gate. The path then goes left to another gate. Go through this

then turn right and continue up the path to the top where another path goes straight across. (NB going left here would take you back into Rearsby, by the village hall). Turn right and you eventually come out on the road at the top of Park Hill.

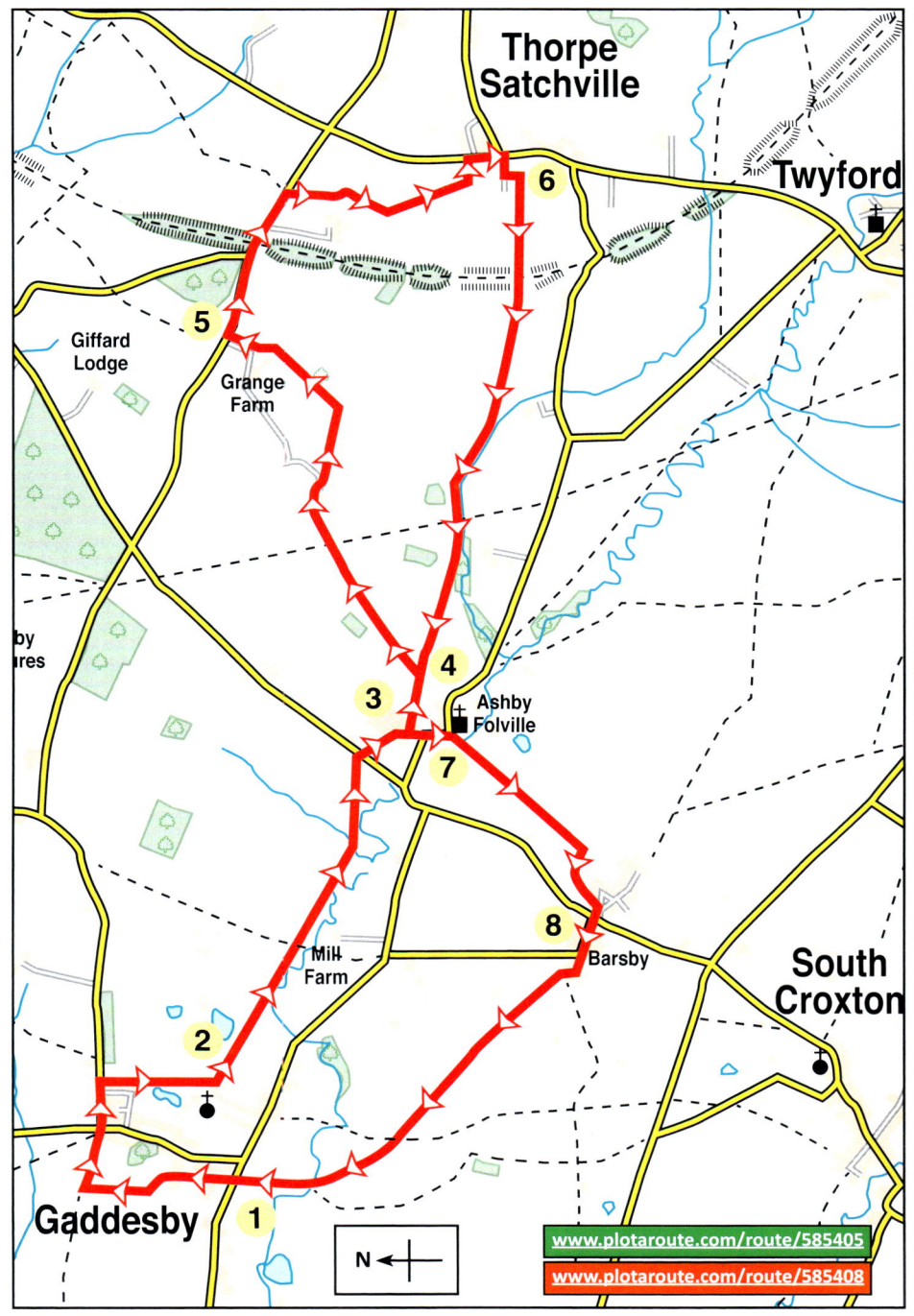

Thorpe
Satchville

Twyford

6

5

Giffard
Lodge

Grange
Farm

4

3

Ashby
Folville

7

Mill
Farm

8

Barsby

South
Croxton

2

Gaddesby

1

N

Cross over and take the road opposite. When the houses finish on your right, there is a footpath to the right which you take. Continue down the field with back gardens on your right. At the bottom there are two metal swing gates and then a stile **2** (C).

Ignore the path that goes straight ahead but instead take the one that goes diagonally left to a gate in the hedge and a small bridge.

Continue to the next gate which follows shortly. Go through a narrow gap in the fence into a large, open field. Head over towards the trees opposite. (The path is just to the left of the trees). Pass to the right of a yellow post (D) and you go through some bushes before you are in open fields once more. The next gate is ahead in front of you and the yellow post is quite visible. You reach another path going across you which is part of the Midshires Way, ignore this and continue straight ahead on the path (which is part of the Leicestershire Round). Notice the disused, decapitated Windmill at Mill Farm on your right. The next obstacle is a stile on the right hand side of a pair of metal bar gates, after this go across the middle of the field to a stile, then slightly left over another field to a metal gate you can see at a gap in the hedge. On entering the next field it is not always obvious where the path goes. You need to cross the field diagonally left to the opposite corner and a gate to get out onto a road. (If this is difficult going, you can turn right and go round the edge of the field to reach the road, and then go left up to where the footpath crosses the road, approximately 100 metres). The path continues across the road slightly to the left. Cross the field heading for a gap between the houses, this comes out on a road in Ashby Folville. **3**

Shorter Route: Turn right down Highfield End to pass the Carington Arms on your left (E). Continue as at **7** below.

Longer Route: Cross over Highfield End and take the stile at the side of the gate, continue up the field with the gardens on your left and then head over the field, slightly right, to a gate in the hedge (ignoring the yellow post and stile on your right). At the time of writing, there was only one arrow pointing straight ahead **4** , but your route goes diagonally left, up the field and passing to the side of the telegraph pole (if this field is difficult to cross due to crops and there is no obvious path, you can go left over to the hedge ahead and then right up the field), the yellow post and gate is by a large tree. The next yellow post can just be seen above the hedge, diagonally right across the field. At this gate, there are two concrete beams for you to cross a small brook, once again the path goes diagonally left up the field but the next gate cannot be seen until you reach the crown of the field. There are now two gates to go through, one either side of the drive to Ashby Grange on

your right. Turning right after the second of these will lead to another gate and then you pass by the gardens and sculptures of the Grange (can you spot who guards the premises? fortunately not alive!). Go down and slightly right to the gate in the bottom corner (F), over

a couple of planks and then diagonally left once more. It appears as though you should head for a large gap in the corner but the yellow post and the stile are just up and left of that. Heading diagonally right now, with Grange Farm in view, look for a yellow post and gate heading into a small copse (G).

The short path to the left through the trees (H) brings you to the side of a farm building (nice view of a lake

over to the right). Go left here (I) to another gate and then slightly right over the field which leads to another gate and out onto the road. **5** Turn right and you will cross a railway line and then take the next footpath on the right.

Go through the small metal swing gate and head down the field with the hedge on your left. The gate is in the bottom left-hand corner and leads to a small wood. You leave the wood and enter a large open field. Continue ahead with

the hedge on your left for about 100 m and then take the double stile on your left (J). You now head diagonally right. The yellow post is to the

left of the central island of trees (see circle on J). The path takes you to the far corner of the field, where you cross a double wooden stile (K), another small field and a gate which takes you out onto the road on the edge of Thorpe Satchville village.

Turn right and then right again into Church Lane **6** - after about one hundred metres turn left into Church Walk. At the church, pass through the small metal gate into the cemetery. When the concrete path swings right, go straight ahead over the grass to a wooden stile. Turn right (not straight ahead) and go alongside a low garden wall. Go through 2 metal gates. Although now not very obvious because of newly created artificial horse fields, your path crosses between these horse fields (L) and gradually descends down, and then swings slightly right to a yellow post and large gate.

From the next small field a stile takes you under a tall brick bridge. After the large gate,

the path is not visible, but you head over the brow to the rise and you are presented with a large field and good views (M). Head across the field to the next gate and a yellow post in the far left hand corner. Again, another large field to cross, in the same direction, to an old wooden gate with two yellow posts to pass by. Continue in a straight line along the bottom of the field with hedges on your left. The next yellow post is on the right hand side of the gap in the hedge. Then another field passing to the left of a pylon leads to a third similar

field. At the end of this field, you need to turn right to reach the next yellow post, where you then turn left. Continue for a short distance, but then take a right fork to climb the hill (N) and pass to the right of a telegraph pole. Over the brow you start to see the houses of Ashby Folville and when you reach the next gate you realise this is where you started the loop over to Thorpe Satchville. Keep straight ahead over

the brow (ignoring a yellow post and stile on your left) and you now come out on the road Highfield End which you were on some time ago, turn left and go down the road past Carington Arms (E) on your left.

7 Follow the road round to the left and then cross over into Church Lane (O). The footpath continues ahead to the right of Brook Cottage, go across a small field towards a drive lined by a low metal fence. Between the trees is a small gate so that you can cross the drive of Ashby Folville Manor. Now proceed up the next two fields and eventually bear half right to a yellow post and gate along the hedge.

Going through this gate takes you into a bush lined path and then right at the bottom and past the tall brick building on your left (P) to enter the village of Barsby.

Built early in the 20th Century, the architect Rev J Godson, originally intended the building to be a mortuary (with no church at Barsby, when a death occurred in the village, the inhabitants had to carry the coffin to the neighbouring village of Ashby Folville), but was not given permission and it became known as Godson's Folly. It was subsequently converted for residential use with the addition of a modern extension and is now known as the Tower House.

The tarmac ahead is Church Lane and this leads to the road Baggrave End. Turn right and straight over the crossroads into Main Street **8** (Q).

"Stoneleigh", situated on Main Street, dates from 1691 and is the oldest building in the village. This is a particularly fine example of the local vernacular, built of red brick with leaded Yorkshire sliding sash windows. Brick detailing in the form of a diaper and checkerboard patterning, divided by a stringcourse, reinforce its attractiveness.

At the end of Main Street where the road bends right is a large house opposite (this was once the King William IV Public House). Take the lane to the left of this house and then, ignoring the footpath straight ahead, swing right onto a footpath track then left through the trees to a gate and into open fields. Go right for a few metres and then left, following a shallow ditch over towards the trees. You pass a small pond on the right and eventually reach a stile and yellow post in the hedge on your right. There are now three more fields with either a stile or a gate.

After this it appears the path goes straight ahead towards a small gap in the hedge but you need to head diagonally left and down to the yellow post which is where the taller hedges finish and there are smaller hedges to the right of

it (R). At the gap, the post seems to send you down the side of the hedge, but instead, cross the narrow brook into the next field, taking care over the electrified fence with an insulated sleeve on it. Turn right towards the yellow post and stile. After crossing this go diagonally left to the yellow post to the left of the tall trees. Cross an old wooden bridge (S) and go between the avenue of trees up to the road in Gaddesby and the Cheney Arms where you started.

Route 10 – Twyford, Burrough on the Hill, Somerby & John O'Gaunt.

Start: Twyford Church, Church Lane, LE14 2HU

Distance: 6.75 miles (shorter option 5.25 miles)

Refreshments: The Saddle Pub in Twyford and Grants Pub in Burrough.

1 Leave Church Lane by walking up Hollow Lane (A). After a short while, take the footpath or the left. Go up a grassy bank to a stile and Yellow Post. The path now veers slightly right to another yellow post between the trees. After this, you are soon aware of a large hollow on your left, keep to the right of this. As you now descend slightly to a wooden gate in the hedge straight in front of you, look ahead and you will see another hedge going away from you along the top of the next field.

Pass through the gate and head up to the hedge and keep it on your right until it ends. There is a yellow post in front of you under a tree **2** (B).

A path also comes up to here from your left, but you need the one that goes right and is usually clearly visible up over the middle of the field. This eventually takes you out on to the road on the outskirts of Burrough on the Hill (C).

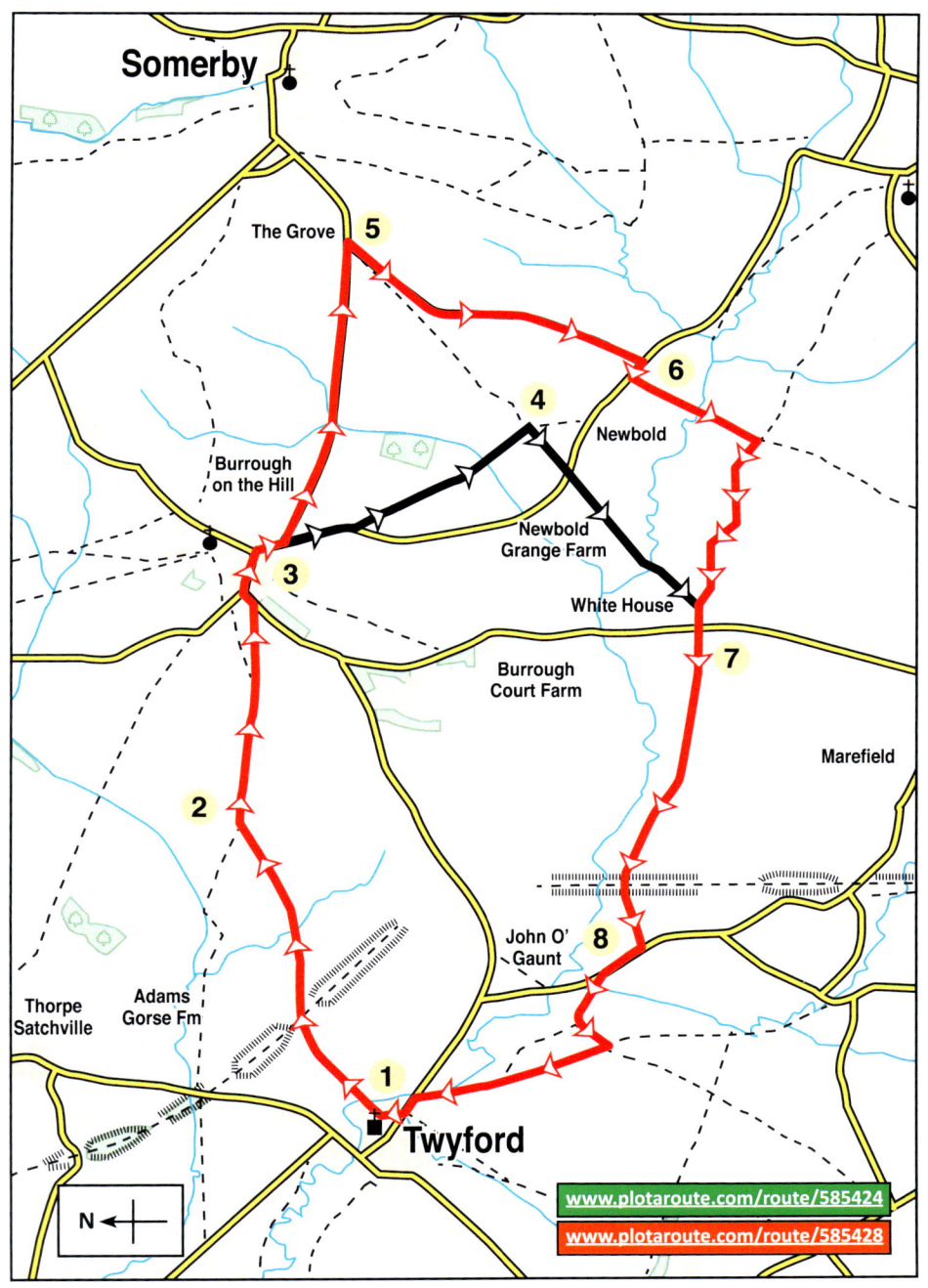

Somerby

The Grove **5**

6

4

Newbold

Burrough
on the Hill

Newbold
Grange Farm

3

White House

Burrough
Court Farm

7

Marefield

2

John O'
Gaunt

8

Thorpe
Satchville

Adams
Gorse Fm

1

Twyford

N

Turn left on the road which then bends right and passes the Grants Pub on your right. When the main road bends left, continue on the road ahead which slopes down **3** .

Shorter route: Continue down the road to where it bends to the right. Take the

footpath on the left into open fields (D). The path descends now and because it is not immediately obvious, head for where there is a break in the hedge ahead and slightly right (E). You now climb gradually towards the trees and hedges that run along the top of the field. Once in the middle of

the field you get to see where the next footpath sign is.

When you reach the top of the fields, you can see there is a track coming from the left from Somerby. Go through a gate to get on the track and turn right here **4** . Keep the hedge on your right to reach the road. Cross over and take the path up to Newbold

Grange Farm (F). Continue across the edge of the field with the hedge on your right. Pass through a pair of gates in the hedge in front of you to get into the next field and continue ahead once more. When you reach a yellow post indicating a path going straight across (NB longer route joins you from the left), turn right to pass some farm buildings to reach a road (Dawson's Lane). Continue at **7** below.

Longer route: Very soon you will see a lane on your left, but the path is to the right of this, with its entrance between 2 wooden fences (G). Continue through the newly

planted trees and soon there is a metal gate on your right which you go through and then left down the field to the next yellow post, at which point there are a couple of wooden steps and a wooden plank bridge to cross. Bear diagonally left again over a large field.

The next brook to cross has a fairly steep path down and another wooden bridge (H). The next 2 yellow posts are up and between 2 bushes (I).

Carry on climbing to reach the fence at the top and

then bear left (J). Further on there is a gate to go through and then continue ahead to a large metal gate

which takes you out on to the road **5** which, if you went left, would lead onto Somerby Village. However you need to go right, away from Somerby (K).

Stay on this road, ignoring a footpath sign on your right, and at the bottom swing right past 'Newbold Farm'.

Immediately after the buildings take the lane on the left **6** (L). This lane changes into a track which goes down to a ford, but there is a wooden bridge on the

left to get across the water (M).

Then continue up the track, but before reaching the top look for 2 yellow posts on your right where a footpath goes straight across (N) – turn right here to walk between the 2 fences. When you can see that this track is about to lead up into 'Owston

Lodge Farm', take the footpath on the right (O) by going through a

metal swing gate over to another yellow post diagonally across this field. Then it is down to another gate to the right and a slight climb to reach the hedge in front of you. Keep this hedge on your right as you head towards 'White House Farm' at the road.

7 The route continues across the road to the left of White House Farm. Proceed along the edge of the field with the hedge on your right. Half way over the field, pass through a gate on your right into the next field (possible horses). Go half left down the basin and up the other side. The gate is at the top, just to the left of a couple of trees. Continuing over the next field, you get your first sight of the splendid Marefield Viaduct (P). Go through the gate in the hedge and then over the brow of the hill.

Marefield Junction was a railway junction. Railway lines from the triangular junction ran westwards to Leicester, northwards to Nottingham and south to Market Harborough. There was never a station at this location, but just to the north was John O'Gaunt railway station; just to the south was Tilton railway station, and just to the west was Lowesby railway station. The line closed to regular passenger trains in December 1953, but retained a healthy goods traffic until 1962. The 14 arch brick viaduct was built for the Great Northern & London & North Western Railway Joint line and opened in 1879.

Bear very slightly to the right, heading for the leftmost arch, where the path goes through this archway. Pass along the edge of the field, by a couple of buildings, to reach Twyford road. Turn right down the road to find the next footpath sign on your left **8** (Q). The path heads diagonally right over the field and the gate is just to the right of where the hedge finishes. Lowenva Lodge is the building on the right. Go straight across the next field, the gate opposite being quite obvious.

The path is now not obvious at all until you head half right over the brow and then you can see a small wooden gate. After going through this gate bear gradually left over to the hedge. Take care not to miss the path when it goes between two hedgerows to another gate. Once through the gate bear half right and you will come out on Burrough Road in Twyford. Turn left, cross over and back to Church Lane where you started.

Interactive Maps

Each of the routes, either the shorter or longer option, are available to view online.

You could also download these from the website to your GPS, Smartphone or Tablet as they are .gpx files, and therefore compatible with most leading mapping software.

Go to www.plotaroute.com/route/nnnnn

Where nnnnn is one of the following codes:-

Route	Shorter	Longer
1	584900	584909
2	584924	-
3	584935	584943
4	617082	617151
5	585356	585381
6	585387	585391
7	585394	585401
8	585442	585445
9	585405	585408
10	585424	585428

Amendments to Volume 1

Route 2.
Construction work is taking place between numbers ⑦ and ⑧ on the route. Old Rise Rocks Cottage has been demolished.

Route 3.
Just after number ⑥ the spot island at Waterside Drive has been removed.

Route 9.
Shorter route – at photo D, the book says go left instead of following the actual path, but this is now fenced off, so you must take the path straight on. It comes out on the road. Go left for a few metres and then left down the track to continue at ⑨.